SOME REFLECTIONS ON THE SELECTION AND
PROMOTION OF JUDGES IN EUROPEAN LAW

SOME REFLECTIONS ON THE SELECTION AND PROMOTION OF JUDGES IN EUROPEAN LAW

FIVE NEXT STEPS IN DEFENCE OF INDEPENDENT JUSTICE

Inaugural speech

Prof. Dr Kees Sterk

Maastricht University

10 March 2023

Published, sold and distributed by Eleven

P.O. Box 85576

2508 CG The Hague

The Netherlands

Tel.: +31 70 33 070 33

Fax: +31 70 33 070 30

e-mail: sales@elevenpub.nl

www.elevenpub.com

Sold and distributed in USA and Canada

Independent Publishers Group

814 N. Franklin Street

Chicago, IL 60610, USA

Order Placement: +1 800 888 4741

Fax: +1 312 337 5985

orders@ipgbook.com

www.ipgbook.com

Eleven is an imprint of Boom uitgevers Den Haag.

ISBN 978-94-6236-529-2

ISBN 978-94-0011-247-6 (E-book)

© 2023 Kees Sterk | Eleven

Cover image: The Judgement of Paris (c. 1636). Oil on oak wood, 144.8 × 193.7 cm (57.0 × 76.3 in). National Gallery, London

TABLE OF CONTENT

1. Introduction   7

2. Three remarks on the context in which the European
   Treaties operate   11

3. European law requirements for the selection and promotion of judges   25

4. Conclusion   41

Notes   47

—

Mr Pro-Rector,

Ladies and gentlemen,

1. INTRODUCTION[1]

It was in the year 2007 that the phone on my desk in my chambers at the Court of Appeal rang. I picked it up and stated my name. The Voice-From-The-Other-Side said, "This is the President of the Supreme Court speaking. You are chosen to be our next member. Do you accept?" I was silent after these few sentences. I did not recognize the tap on my shoulder at first. To be honest, my first thoughts were that my dear colleagues were pulling my leg as they had done before. This time, however, it was different: I did not recognize one of their voices. So, I decided to be cautious in answering: "I am sorry, Mr President, but I do not recollect applying for the job." "That is correct," the Voice retorted, "we do not do applications." The rest is history.

That was the Netherlands in 2007, and, to be fair, since then the selection of Supreme Court judges has seen some changes. Now, the Court does some kind of application process via advertisements,[2] with interviews of candidates, and two lay people, experts in human resources, are involved in the selection process.[3] The Dutch government supports amending the Dutch Constitution on the selection and appointment of judges to the Supreme Court.[4] In other words, the subject of selection of Supreme Court judges in the Netherlands is in motion.

And the Netherlands is not the only country in Europe where this subject is being debated: more and more discussions are being held in more European countries, usually connected with the independence of the judiciary. The subject of these discussions is not just the selection of apex court judges but, more widely, the selection of judges at all levels. Some European countries have changed their selection processes for national judges.[5] Some of those changes have been the subject of comment and criticism from the European Commission, the European Parliament, the Venice Commission or other European organizations. A by-now tsunami of cases has even led to judgments by the European courts in Luxembourg and Strasbourg, and there are more to come.

National judges in Europe appear critical of their national selection processes, as shown in ENCJ surveys over the past seven years. In these surveys, national judges across Europe responded to questions regarding the selection and promotion of judges in their countries. The results are worrying, not just in Central European countries[6] but also in other parts of Europe. As an example, I will mention some of the results of the latest ENCJ Survey on the Independence of Judges (2022).

Responding to a question on first appointments,[7] there were only a few judiciaries in which over 90% of respondents believed that judges were selected solely on the basis of ability and experience. That is the case in Denmark, the Netherlands and Northern Ireland. In other judiciaries, large numbers of respondents believed that judges are not selected solely on the basis of merit and experience: 35% in Bosnia and Herzegovina, 39% in Croatia, 42% in Hungary and 32% in Bulgaria.

The responses to questions about promotion of judges from first instance and appellate courts[8] drew more negative responses than those for first appointments. An average of 20% of respondents believed strongly that judges are promoted other than on the basis of ability and experience, with almost 40% of respondents in Hungary, Italy, Portugal and Spain responding negatively.

The results are as bad, or even worse, for the question regarding selection for appointment to apex courts.[9] 65% of respondents from Spain and 52% from Hungary expressed the opinion that these appointments are not based only on ability and experience, and in Germany (34%), Italy (36%) and Portugal (38%), too, the percentages are high.

On the basis of all this, one might conclude that the selection processes for national judges in Europe raise doubts whether they always provide reliable means of identifying persons who possess the right qualities for a judge. In today's inaugural speech at Maastricht University, in grateful acceptance of the newly created chair of Administration of European Justice, I intend to give the subject some attention.

I will focus on the issues of initial appointments and promotion of judges to Courts of Appeal and Supreme Courts, because, in my view, the key to long-term political control over the judiciary lies in political dominance over the selection and appointment processes for judges and Court Presidents.[10]

I will begin with three remarks on the European context in which judiciaries have to operate: attacks on national judges acting as European judges, the ineffective enforcement of Union standards regarding the independence of the judiciary, and the many different national contexts Europe has. To be followed by the heart of the matter: the European law requirements for selecting judges and Presidents. In that respect I will touch upon subjects like the objective criteria on merit, moral integrity and courage, the European standard for selection bodies for judges and Presidents: majority of judges elected by their peers, undue influence of politicians or judges organizations over these bodies and, finally, the limits of discretionary power of the executive regarding recommendations of selection bodies. I will end my speech by identifying five next steps that, in my opinion, are necessary in defence of independent European justice.

2. THREE REMARKS ON THE CONTEXT IN WHICH THE EUROPEAN TREATIES OPERATE

2.1 INTRODUCTION

Both the European Convention on Human Rights (the Convention) and the European Union Treaties (Union law) require that European law[11] is applied uniformly. For the functioning of the Treaties it is vital that European judges are independent.[12] Because almost all European judges are selected by national selection processes, the national processes of selecting judges must also serve the purpose of selecting independent European judges. Therefore, it is important to know the selection rules and how these rules work out in the national practice. This can only be done within the context of the countries in which the selection rules operate. That is why I will start my speech by briefly touching upon three important contexts in Europe that influence the selection rules for European judges. First, governmental attacks on independent judges acting as European judges. Second, the European Commission's systemic non-effective enforcement of standards concerning judicial independence in the Union. And, finally, the existence of different contexts in the European countries as to history, culture, legal systems and concepts.

2.2 ATTACKS ON NATIONAL JUDGES ACTING AS EUROPEAN JUDGES

I will now take you back in time to the atrocities of World War II. They had many causes. Two of them were the non-functioning of an independent judiciary in the Weimar Republic[13] and the dehumanization of groups of persons in Nazi Germany that followed. To prevent this kind of catastrophe ever happening again, either caused by fascism or communism, countries decided to create an international system intended to safeguard peace and justice by means of a rule-based order that effectively protects everyone's fundamental rights.

In line with this idea, the Council of Europe and the European Union were founded. The Council of Europe produced the Convention. In essence, this Convention guarantees fundamental rights to every person in Europe, protected by a right to a fair trial before independent national courts, while the European Court of Human Rights in Strasbourg is designated as the ultimate arbiter of these rights. The European Union is not a party to this Convention, but the rights in the Charter of Fundamental Rights of the Union on the independence of the judiciary have the same meaning and scope as those in the Convention.[14] Therefore, it is not surprising that both Courts work closely together in the developing of standards of judicial independence.[15] The application of these rights in case law is done by national judges acting as European judges.

Over the years the case law of the Courts has affected more and more areas of domestic law in countries which are party to the Treaties. In some of these areas, especially in immigration law, environmental law and the law regarding the organization of the national judiciaries, a number of European governments vehemently oppose this case law, essentially because it prevents them from implementing freely their policies or ideas in these fields. There are, of course, many different explanations for this phenomenon, all very interesting and important, but I will hold back on this issue, because the explanations are not really important for the issue at hand that the phenomenon of national opposition to European case law undermines the effectiveness of the international rule-based system for justice and peace.

The most annihilating strategy is that of Russia. On 24 February 2022, this became very clear when Russia invaded Ukraine, and thus – in line with the ideas behind this invasion – departed completely from the rule-based system of peace and justice in Europe.[16] But the strategies of other governments in countries like Poland and Hungary are disastrous as well. They have a strategy of remaining party to the Treaties, probably for financial reasons, but by so-called 'judicial reforms' both countries have significantly undermined the European systems' key concept that national judiciaries must be independent for the system to be effective. As a result, in Poland, the Constitutional Tribunal has held that all the case laws of both European Courts concerning the requirements for the independence of the judiciary are null and void in the Polish national legal order.[17] Another Polish instrument for undermining the independence of the Polish judiciary is that of disciplining judges who apply the Treaties[18] or exerting political control in the selection of national judges.[19]

A third strategy is from the United Kingdom, different in nature, but still dangerous to the system. In 2020, the UK left the Union, but is still a party to the Convention. However, it is unilaterally trying to change its effectiveness by national legislation reducing the influence of the judgments of the Strasbourg Court on national UK-judges judgments.[20] In the words of Lord Dyson: "… some of the provisions of the Bill, if enacted, would materially diminish human rights protection."[21]

2.3 SYSTEMIC ENFORCEMENT GAP IN UNION STANDARDS REGARDING THE INDEPENDENCE OF THE JUDICIARY

Both Treaties essentially rely on national enforcement by countries who are party to one or both Treaties.[22] The Commission is a pivotal enforcer of Union law within the Union. It has many instruments with which to do so, including launching infringement actions,[23] applying penalty payments[24] in case of noncompliance with judgments of the Luxembourg Court and making the independence of the judiciary a precondition for payments from Union Funds.[25] I want to briefly point out two aspects of enforcement by the Commission: the discretionary power to launch infringement actions and the discretionary power to enforce judgments of the Luxembourg Court in the field of the independence of the judiciary.

2.3.1 Discretionary power to launch infringement actions

The first point concerns the Commission's exercise of its power to launch infringement actions to stop and reverse the attacks on judicial independence in some Member States. Since Hungary started so-called judicial reforms in 2010, followed by Poland in 2015, the Commission's first approach stopping this backsliding of the rule of law was technical with a narrow scope.[26] Between 2012 and 2017, the Commission did not pursue any infringement action more or less explicitly concerned with the protection of judicial independence.[27] In 2018, after a landmark judgment by the Luxembourg Court, the number and scope of infringement actions increased a bit but "has not fundamentally altered the situation on the ground".[28] The same still goes for the decision by the European Council of freezing money payable by the Union to Hungary if this country does not meet four, rather abstract, conditions on judicial independence.[29] Whether it will change the situation on the ground depends on the assessment of those vague conditions by the Commission in the future.

The Commission has acknowledged the ineffectiveness of its enforcement strategy and explains it either as resulting from a lack of necessary tools to defend judicial independence or that it could not afford to lose a case before the Luxembourg Court or that it had other important crises at hand.[30] In his 2022 inaugural lecture, Morijn addressed the issue and is very clear: "No, there is no problem of too few instruments." On the contrary: "it is mostly a problem of using tools that are effective to confront illiberal national governments…, and simply not using other potentially effective options that are available already".[31]

In my own words: it is not a lack of instruments that is holding back the Commission, but a lack of legal courage and a lack of political will. As an explanation for the lack of political will, Keleman and Pavone[32] argue that the Commission is afraid of losing intergovernmental support for its policy proposals if it were to enforce the standards aggressively. Grainne De Burca explains that one of the reasons for the Commission not to confront Poland and Hungary is that it believes it can contain the effects of a lack of independent judiciaries in those countries.[33]

Of course, it is important to establish exactly how these elements contribute to the ineffective enforcement of the standards for the independence of the judiciary. However, it is now without doubt that (geo)politics plays a big part in it. The 2022 Union decision to unblock EUR 36 million to Poland under conditions not addressing the on-going destruction of judicial independence in that country, clearly shows[34] this: the Union valued its unity against Russia more than the protection of Polish independent judges.[35] And for geopolitical reasons Ukraine, Moldova and Bosnia Herzegovina are now officially given candidate status, although nobody doubts that in all these countries the independence of the judiciary is not yet up to European standards.[36]

From a geopolitical point of view, this might be wise, but this role of the Commission, prioritizing geopolitics over compliance with the Charter's and Treaties' duty to uphold the standards of the independence of the judiciary, especially to systemic infringements such as in Hungary and Poland,[37] causes a systemic enforcement gap regarding an issue that is fundamental to the identity and functioning of the Union. Because of this systemic gap, I raise the question whether it is still justifiable that the Commission should mainly have the power to launch infringement actions to protect the independence of the judiciary. The danger of not filling the gap is that, over the long term, it undermines the very identity and functioning of the Union as a union of democratic countries under the rule of law. The paradox of defending our very identity as democracies under the rule of law against Russia while in the process destroying independent judiciaries within the Union itself is in urgent need of resolution. Is part of solving this paradox the creation of an (a) political body tasked with the duty to defend the independence of the judiciary to (also) launch infringement actions in defence of independent justice? Or, are other solutions possible?

2.3.2 *Discretionary power to enforce judgments of the courts*

This brings me to my second point: the discretionary power to enforce judgments of the Courts on judicial independence. This point needs some introduction. As of 1 January 2021, the Union established a new instrument for enforcing the rule of law: it made the independence of the judiciary[38] a precondition for payments from Union Funds.[39] As a result of this instrument, Poland's EUR 36 billion from the National Recovery and Resilience Plan were frozen. On 17 June 2022, the European Council approved a Commission proposal to release that money, provided Poland implemented three milestones.[40]

Shockingly enough, the duty to reform the selection body for judges is not one of the milestones, although Strasbourg case law is extremely explicit that this body is politically dominated. Is the reason for this omission that only the Strasbourg Court is explicit in its case law on this issue, and not the Luxembourg Court? If so, that would deny the Union law rule, in existence for many years now, that the rights on judicial independence in Union law have the same meaning and scope as those in the Convention. In other words, the case law of the Strasbourg Court as to the systemic lack of independence of judges is part of Union law.[41] In my opinion, the duty to reform the selection body for judges should clearly have been one of the milestones, because a politically dominated selection body for judges is most important for a long-term political control of the judiciary by the executive.

Back to the milestones. One of them is the reinstatement of Polish judges, suspended unlawfully by the 'Disciplinary Chamber' of the Polish Supreme Court. In the agreement between the

Commission and Poland, this milestone is elaborated as a procedure of review of the status of the suspended judges, lasting at least a year or more, without guaranteeing the result of reinstatement of those judges. This milestone is obviously contrary to the judgment of the Luxembourg Court[42] requiring Poland to reinstate the judges at once, without any review, and is an example of the Commission not enforcing strongly the judgments of the Luxemburg Court as to judicial independence. It again shows the danger of the Commission having discretionary power for enforcing clear judgments on issues fundamental to the identity and functioning of the Union.

One of the requirements of the rule of law is that the executive must enforce the judgments of independent courts. Therefore, the systemic enforcement gap should be remedied. The Luxembourg Court may contribute to filling the gap by introducing a strict duty on the Commission (and other Union Institutions) to enforce these judgments in full, without delay and by all available instruments.[43] It could introduce such a duty, considering that the systemic gap emerged for political reasons in the last decade was never intended in the Treaties in the first place[44] and that the subject relates to an issue fundamental to the identity and functioning of the Union. In this regard, the Court may also consider that a duty to enforce judgments of the Court already exists as to acts of Union Institutions declared null and void.[45] In my opinion, the reasons for a strict duty to enforce judgments on judicial independence are at least equally important to the functioning of the Union as the reasons underlying the existing duty. The Court could look at the duty not to act on an act declared null and void as a negative duty to uphold the Union system, and the duty to enforce judgments on the independence of the judiciary as a positive duty to do the same.

Another way to ensure that Union Institutions enforce judgments of the Courts concerning the independence of the judiciary is to grant interested parties, such as representatives of European judiciaries – the Strasbourg Court labelled them 'rule of law watchdogs'[46] – access to the Luxembourg Court. This is the goal of the law suit being launched on 27 August 2022 by four European judicial organizations.[47] In the light of the systemic enforcement gap, that action provides the Court with the opportunity to take a next, in my view, necessary step to ensure legal protection in Union law, where the European Commission and Council are failing in their enforcement duty.

I conclude that the Commission's geopolitical role has caused a systemic enforcement gap as to Union law on judicial independence, which was not intended by the Treaties. This endangers the identity and functioning of the Union. Because, furthermore, the rule of law requires the executive to enforce the judgments of independent courts, this gap should be remedied. In my opinion, additional enforcement mechanisms must be considered.

2.4 THE MANY DIFFERENT NATIONAL CONTEXTS IN EUROPE

European countries differ substantially as to their economic and social development, as well as their history, legal culture and legal concepts. Different contexts may result in European standards appearing to operate differently in various countries. This must be remembered when assessing the application of standards to (selection processes for) independent judges in Europe. In consequence, a comparison of European standards solely on the basis of the text of domestic law alone may give distorted results. Or, in the words of the Consultative Council of European Judges

(CCJE), "formal rules alone do not guarantee that appointment decisions are taken impartially, according to objective criteria and free from political influence."[48] This method is therefore usually not sufficient or often creates confusion.

The Courts recognize this issue, for instance when applying a rule of domestic law that the executive may refuse a candidate selected by a selection body. They consider how often the executive applies the rule and in what circumstances.[49]

I will now clarify my point by some examples in the field of selection of judges.

The first example is about the same rule in some countries that a decision to appoint a judge has to be signed by the executive. This rule exists both in Poland and the Netherlands: the decision to appoint a judge has to be signed by the President of the Republic (Poland) or by the King and Minister of Justice (the Netherlands). However, this rule operates quite differently as to the independence of judges. In 2015 and 2016, the President of the Polish Republic used this rule to effectively refuse to sign 11 appointment decisions for judges who were, at the time, rightfully selected by the selection body.[50] He did not even give reasons for it.[51] His motives are widely seen as political because he saw the selected candidates as political enemies.[52] In the Netherlands, the King and the Minister of Justice have to sign the decision, but they do not use it to refuse candidates, let alone on political grounds. Apparently the same rule, but not quite, and with a totally different result from the point of view of judicial independence.

A second example: the active involvement of a Minister of Justice in the selection of Court Presidents. The Polish government justified the active involvement of the Minister of Justice in the selection of Court Presidents by referring to the active involvement of Ministers of Justice in Germany. However, the powers of Court Presidents in Poland and Germany differ quite substantially as to the possibility and practice that a Court President influences the outcome of court cases. Presidents of Polish courts have almost unlimited power to compose panels, to assign cases to these panels or to transfer judges, while German Presidents are bound by the composition of the Senates of the court and the assignment rules for these Senates. Furthermore, the transfer of a judge can be appealed to a committee of judges of the court which can overrule the decision of the President. In other words, for a German President, it is difficult to influence the outcome of cases pending before the court by using Presidential powers, but not for a Polish President and he or she uses these powers to do so.[53] The context of these different powers of presidents in both countries makes the active involvement of the Minister of Justice in Poland unacceptable from the point of view of judicial independence, and the active involvement of Ministers of Justice in Germany probably undesirable from the same perspective, but not unacceptable, as long as the guarantees against political influence in the outcome of specific court cases function well.

A third example: the same European standards of independence of selection bodies of judges are sometimes guarantee enough to select independent judges, and sometimes not. After the change in 1989 in some European countries from a communist system of government to a system of democracy under the rule of law, the task of selecting judges in the new order was usually given to councils for the judiciary. These councils were established according to the various recommendations of the Council of

Europe (CCJE and Venice Commission), the European Network of Councils for the Judiciary (ENCJ) and the Organization for Security and Co-operation in Europe, Office for Democratic Institutions and Human Rights (OSCE-ODIHR).[54] These organizations all recommended that the councils should be independent from the executive and that they should have a majority of judges chosen by their peers. The idea behind this was that independent selection bodies were best placed to identify independent judges. Now, many years later, some independent bodies seem to have corrupted this concept. For instance, in the use, or, one might also say misuse by judges in the selection bodies to influence judges in individual cases: some councillors are said to indicate informally to judges that if they want a promotion, they have to decide an important case in a certain way.[55] When exposed, these corrupt councillors usually claim protection from the independence of the selection body and are sometimes – in practice – untouchable because of this protection. In these situations, European standards intended to promote independence turn against their purpose. Solutions for these situations have to be found, without destroying the independence of the judiciary. Establishing a culture of accountability of the judiciary is in my view one of the main promising policies to tackle this problem.[56]

To conclude, European standards on the selection of independent judges have to operate in different national contexts. For that reason it is essential that the objective pursued by the standards is effectively attained. Sometimes this result may be achieved, even though the standard appears to be applied somewhat differently. Sometimes, the context in a country requires this different application to serve the effective attainment of the object of such standard. For lawyers who consider the law just as a dogmatic system of rules, and are not trained 'to broaden the law from within', as Twining advocated in his book – Law in Context: Enlarging a Discipline,[57] – this might be challenging, but in my view it is the only way. A strict, dogmatic approach cannot serve Europe in this field. This makes the comparison of selection systems for judges in Europe not easy, but all the more interesting. A lot of research has to be done in this field, especially as to how selection procedures actually operate.

3. EUROPEAN LAW REQUIREMENTS FOR THE SELECTION AND PROMOTION OF JUDGES

I will now go to the heart of the matter: the legal requirements for the selection and promotion of judges. To position these rules, and explain their nature, I will start with three introductory remarks.

3.1 THREE INTRODUCTORY REMARKS

First of all, the European courts do not deal with every irregularity in selection processes for judges: this is subsidiarity in action. As a rule, the Strasbourg Court only interferes when three conditions are met:

1. A manifest breach of domestic law, established by a national court;
2. The breach must pertain to a fundamental rule of the selection procedure;
3. No effective remedy is provided by domestic courts.[58]

However, in the event that domestic law is incompatible with the object and purpose of the Convention,[59] or a judgment of a domestic court is arbitrary or manifestly unreasonable,[60] the Court will consider the case even if there is no manifest breach of domestic law. With these rules, the Strasbourg Court does not seek to redesign national judiciaries.[61] The same goes for the Luxemburg Court: it limits itself to examining whether rules that concern the organization and functioning of national courts comply with the principle of judicial independence.[62]

The most fundamental point is that the requirements for the independence of the judiciary are sufficiently clear as to the results. I fully agree with Pech[63] on this. So, the history, culture or legal system of a European country can never be a justification not to fulfil its duty to achieve an independent judiciary; the history, culture or legal system of a country are only relevant for answering the question as to which instruments are best suited to fulfil this duty. Sometimes, politicians or diplomats seem to forget this and use cultural or economic reasons to lower the legal requirements for some countries. This forgetfulness is, however, dangerously wrong: the requirements of the independence of the judiciary are European law in force and must therefore be applied and enforced as such.[64]

A third remark is that the legal requirement of judicial independence remains in force, no matter how many or what competences the Member States have referred to the Union. I will explain this a little bit more. Some constitutional courts feel that the Luxembourg Court is creating more and more powers for the Union and want to stop this trend.[65] In political circles, the level of integration is hotly debated. I will not go into the merits of the discussions, but the point is that no matter what level of integration Member States agree to in the Union, at every agreed level, the Union needs the independence of national judiciaries to function well, because the Union is founded on the concept that Union law is applied uniformly in every Member State.

3.2 EUROPEAN LEGAL REQUIREMENTS FOR SELECTION AND APPOINTMENT OF JUDGES

The selection and appointment processes are aimed at identifying persons who possess the right qualities for a judge, as required by European law (independence and impartiality), and doing so in a manner that is legitimate in order to sustain public confidence in the judiciary. I will now engage in identifying and discussing the factors in the case law of both Courts relevant in attaining that purpose. First, the criteria for selection, and change thereof, followed by some procedural aspects of the selection process. Of course, I fully realize that the Courts consider all relevant factors individually yet assess all these factors holistically.[66] Once the Court has established – on the basis of this holistic approach – that there is not 'a tribunal established by law' in the meaning of Article 6 ECHR, it does not require a separate analysis of the overall fairness of the proceedings to the parties involved.[67]

3.2.1 Objective criteria on merit, moral integrity and courage

The first question to ask is what are the right qualities for judges, required by European law? The Strasbourg Court mentions merit, moral integrity[68] and technical competence to protect the rule of law.[69] It holds that the higher the position in the judicial hierarchy, the more demanding the applicable selection criteria should be.[70] It emphasizes the paramount importance of a rigorous process for the selection of judges to ensure that the most qualified candidates are appointed.

The problem with these selection criteria is that European countries do not have a common definition or a common tradition for the role of a judge in society. Some regard judging as a job. In that case, only professional legal competence is relevant. Some look upon it primarily as a public function, which requires competences to be able to engage in more social and political dimensions.[71] Some countries stress the necessity of efficiency in the administration of justice: judging as a service to the public.

England and Wales, for instance, have a policy to further diversity[72] in the judiciary as a quality requirement.[73] In that situation, diversity is not a question of merit of an individual judge, but a quality requirement of the judiciary as a whole. Merit and diversity seem to conflict somehow in selection processes. Since 2013, for instance, the Judicial Appointment Commission in England and Wales has a duty to consider diversity by equal merit. Parliament, however, recently complained that the pace of change was too slow.[74] Gee and Rackley argue that part of the explanation for this slow pace might be merit requirements which advantage 'male and pale' candidates and disadvantage candidates from non-traditional backgrounds. As an example, they cite the requirement for fee-paid experience in a part-time judicial position while continuing in practice.[75]

The different views on the role of a judge/the judiciary of course impact the question who should be members of a selection body. the Netherlands, for instance, has the view that judging is also a service to society and that diversity of the judiciary furthers the quality of the judiciary. But in the Dutch selection system, society is only represented in the body for initial selection of judges, while the bodies selecting for promotions consist only of judges without any representation of society. This is unlike England and Wales, where a lay member of the Judicial Appointment Commission is a voting member in selection bodies for promotions.[76]

Until now, the Courts have mostly left the specific selection criteria to domestic law. This will probably remain so for some time until a common tradition has been established in this field, provided countries establish objective criteria in domestic law and show that they act upon them,[77] unless, of course, domestic law is not compatible with the object and purpose of the Convention.[78] In that case, the Courts will step in. Later on, I will give you some examples of domestic law that the Courts might consider to be incompatible with European law.

3.2.2 *Changing the objective criteria for selection*

Objective selection criteria in domestic law may be changed. This does not have to create a problem for the independence of the judiciary, but it might well be so, where these changes are such that – considering all relevant factors – they give rise to reasonable doubt, in the minds of individuals, as to undue influence of the executive and/or the legislature.[79]

In 2019, in Hungary, for instance, the criteria for selecting Supreme Court judges were changed such that members from the Constitutional Court, who are appointed by the Hungarian Parliament, do not have to fulfil the requirements imposed for other candidates for that position. A year later, the legal requirements for selecting the President of the Supreme Court were changed as well: from then on, time served in the Constitutional Court must be taken into account when calculating the required five years of experience as a judge. As a result, as of 1 January 2021, a new President was appointed by the Hungarian Parliament. There was no judicial involvement in the procedure whatsoever. On the same date, the President of the Supreme Court received additional powers to set up judicial panels for certain groups of cases, appointing presiding judges, assigning judges to chambers and establishing the case allocation scheme among chambers.[80] In my opinion, this set of events will undoubtedly give rise to reasonable doubt in the minds of individuals that the executive is in the process of taking over the Supreme Court. Therefore, domestic law will probably be held incompatible with European law and the appointment of the President of the Supreme Court might well be in violation of European law.

Another example, in 2020, in Germany, the Federal Minister of Justice changed the selection criteria for presiding judges in the federal courts: five years' experience in these courts was no longer required. He did this after the call for the vacancy was made, and he appointed candidates without five years' experience. No doubt, this raises the question whether the executive had undue influence over the selection process. A case is pending before a German court.[81]

3.2.3 The standard for selection bodies: majority of judges, elected by their peers

Both European political and judicial organizations[82] hold that selection bodies for judges should be composed at least half by judges who are elected by their peers, to guarantee the independence of the body from the executive and the legislature.

In three cases against Poland,[83] the Strasbourg Court held that the Polish selection body for judges lacked sufficient guarantees of independence from the legislature and the executive,[84] although it had a majority of judges. One of the reasons was that the judges in the selection body were not elected by their peers but, instead, were appointed by the Polish Parliament. As to the selection process, the Court established that the executive proposed – directly or indirectly – most of the candidates while they were subordinate to the executive and that there were doubts whether all appointed judges had fulfilled the requirement of domestic law to be supported by 25 active judges. As to the acts of the newly composed selection body, it mentioned that international organizations unanimously stated that the selection body had not acted in accordance with the constitutional duty of safeguarding the independence of the judiciary.[85] In accordance with its traditional methodology, the Court assessed these circumstances as a whole and held that there was undue influence by the legislature and executive.[86]

The results of these judgments are to be welcomed. In the future, however, a more strict reasoning by the Court is needed in my view. For instance, judgments based on a presumption that disregarding the European standard 'elected by their peers' establishes undue influence by other state powers, unless proven otherwise. For two reasons this would give effect to a changing context in Europe. First, the unanimous support by the most important European political and judicial organizations for the standard. But more important, the fact that more and more countries are changing domestic law – Luxembourg[87] and Czechia[88] are recent examples – to comply with the standard, while already quite a lot of European countries – especially in the Union – are in compliance with it. In other words, a new European common constitutional tradition in the Union is rapidly being established.

I am fully aware this will likely have consequences for countries not yet in compliance with the standard. Spain, for instance, will have to prove that the selection by the Spanish

Parliament of judges on the selection body for judges does not lead to undue influence of the executive or legislature over the selection process of judges. This proof will probably not be easy to deliver, since the Spanish Parliament has not been able to select judges in the selection body since 2018, because the selection process has been politicized to the core.[89] However, once a new European common constitutional tradition is established, the European Courts will have to give effect to that tradition.

3.2.4   Selection of Court Presidents

Court Presidents have various competences in Europe, but usually they have some influence on the composition of panels of judges, on appointing presiding judges, on assigning judges to chambers, on case allocation, on the transfer of judges, on the promotion of judges and on initiating disciplinary charges against judges. These powers may be used and in some countries are being used to exert pressure to gain political control over judges.[90] Poland is the most open and brutal example of this pressure,[91] but in other countries, like Hungary, it is more hidden and villainous.[92]

The fact that Court Presidents may potentially influence judicial independence is in my opinion all the more reason to apply the standard that the selection body must consist of a majority of judges elected by their peers. This is another example of the Courts having to judge whether domestic law is compatible with the object and purpose of the Convention.[93]

Another example of this sort is most certainly the Polish law on the ordinary courts. In 2017, this law was changed, giving the Minister of Justice the power – for six months – to fire Court

Presidents at will, and to appoint new Presidents without the involvement of any selection body.[94] On 13 February 2018, the Minister of Justice dismissed 137 Presidents and Vice-Presidents of ordinary courts and started appointing new Presidents.[95]

In Hungary, the selection system for Court Presidents theoretically involves judges, but the system in practice bypasses the involvement of judges. I will explain how this works. In each court, its judges vote on candidates for the presidency of that court and inform the executive[96] of the ranking. The executive may deviate from the ranking but is not allowed to appoint a candidate who did not receive a majority of votes of the judges in that court, unless with the consent of the Council for the Judiciary.[97] Whenever the executive does not like the outcome of the selection process, and knows it will not get the majority vote in the Council for the Judiciary, it annuls the selection process and appoints ad interim Presidents, year on year, without any involvement of judges. This has been going on for years now, creating a practice of systemically bypassing ordinary processes of selecting Court Presidents,[98] and giving the executive an enormous influence on such Presidents, and through them on judges, because ad interim Presidents have to be reappointed every year.

In Austria, Presidents of administrative courts are selected by the Minister of Justice, without any judicial involvement whatsoever.[99] In January 2022, some so-called side letters were published, in which the parties to the coalition government agreed that appointments to top-level positions, including the judiciary, were to be divided between the different political parties. An obvious breach of European law as to the rule that the selection of judges should be based on merit, the more so in case of the selection of Presidents.

I conclude this paragraph by reiterating my opinion that in the near future a new European common constitutional tradition will emerge that judges are to be selected by a body composed of a majority of judges, elected by their peers. Once established, the Courts will have to give effect to that tradition. The effect might be that undue influence of the executive is presumed where the selection was not in compliance with this tradition. The same goes, even more so, for the selection of Presidents, because they have powers to influence judges in the outcome of cases. These three examples show how necessary this presumption is for upholding the independence of the judiciary.

3.2.5 Selection bodies under undue influence of judges associations

Not only the executive and the legislature may unduly influence the selection process of judges. The Strasbourg Court recognizes that arbitrary interference in the appointment process may also come from other sources than the legislature and the executive.[100] A 2019 example is the undue influence of judges associations on the selection of high-ranking judicial officers.[101] Some judges, members of the selection body and members of the Italian Parliament were taped, discussing and negotiating the appointments to high positions. It appeared that groups within the National Judges Association[102] had divided important positions in the judiciary, not on the basis of merit, but also on the basis of loyalty to the group, obviously in violation of domestic and European law. The background of this practice was that a candidate for the selection body, usually only locally known, could only be successful in the election by his peers in a big country like Italy, with the support of a national group. Once elected, the judge felt he or she had to be grateful to his or her group by supporting its candidates in selection procedures. The Italian legislature recently adopted a law which changed the election system for judges in the selection body.[103] Before the new law, Italy was one big constituency for electing judges; after the law, Italy is divided in four constituencies. With this change, the Italian legislator expects to have reduced the influence of groups within judges' associations on the selection of judges for high judicial office.

I choose this example to illustrate, once again, that – contrary to what a lot of European judges feel – the danger for judicial independence might not solely come from other state powers but may also come from within the judiciary. I have already mentioned the example of corrupt members of selection bodies.

3.2.6   Selection decisions must be reasoned

Some European countries have a constitutional tradition, like Georgia, that constitutional bodies do not have to reason decisions. In 2020, the Constitutional Court of Georgia held that this rule also applied to the constitutional selection body for judges.[104] The effect of this ruling is that the result of the selection process is not transparent, while a lack of transparency might undermine the trust of citizens in the judiciary. To improve transparency, OSCE-ODIHR proposes to complement the Kyiv Recommendations[105] with a standard of demonstrating to society that objective criteria of appointment are seen to be applied by reasoned decisions.[106] In the event that domestic law, like in Georgia, does not require reasoned decisions by selection bodies, the Strasbourg Court will not be able to fulfil the task of assessing whether the object and purpose of the Convention is being attained. Because it has a duty to assess, in my view, it will impose a duty so to reason decisions of selection bodies.

3.2.7 *The duty of the executive towards recommendations by selection bodies*

A decisive power for the executive in the process of appointing judges does not necessarily give rise to legitimate doubt, in the minds of individuals, as to the imperviousness of appointed judges to influence from the executive as to the neutrality vis-à-vis the interests before them.[107] However, in certain circumstances, the exercise of power by the executive may give rise to such doubt.

Some European judges find this rule disappointing and would rather see a duty for the executive to follow the recommendation of the selection body,[108] full stop. It is a tempting view, because there are quite a few European examples of misuse of power by the executive. Despite the examples, I am not entirely sure I agree. The reason is that in normal and healthy relations between the state powers, the involvement of the executive in the selection processes for judges may contribute to the quality of the selection process.[109] And, as I mentioned earlier, the danger of undermining the independence of the judiciary might well come from inside the judiciary, the more so when the judiciary closes itself off from the influence of other state powers and society. In my opinion, some checks and balances are in order.

What circumstances have to be considered in assessing the doubts mentioned in this paragraph? I will mention seven.

1. The executive has no power to refuse
An example from Poland. Candidates for the Constitutional Tribunal were elected by the Polish Parliament in accordance with domestic law. The domestic rule being that a Parliament had the power to elect these candidates when the term of office of that Parliament covered the date on which the seat became vacant. The President of the Republic, however, refused to swear in these duly elected candidates, but swore in candidates for the same seats, elected by a later Parliament. The Strasbourg Court ruled that he did not have the power to refuse the duly elected candidates, because he was duty-bound to swear them in on the basis of the Polish Constitution.[110]

2. The executive refuses without respecting domestic law as to the objective criteria[111]
In Iceland, the selection body for judges proposed to the Minister of Justice 15 best-ranked candidates for the position of judge in the Court of Appeal. The Minister did not follow the selection body in 4 cases and replaced them by 4 other candidates who were not among the 15 best-ranked candidates. The Minister reasoned the decision by arguing that the selection body had not given enough weight to the domestic law criterion of judicial experience and had had regard to subjective factors as to the success of a candidate in his or her career. The Strasbourg Court ruled that the absence of any further explanation as to how she had measured 'success', or any comparison of all candidates from that perspective, called into question the objectivity of the selection process.[112]

3. The executive refuses without considering the opinion of an
   independent body for selecting judges[113]

Another example from Poland. On 28 June 2016, the President
of the Republic refused to appoint 11 judges who were selected
by a selection body with a majority of judges, elected by their
peers.[114] A case is pending before the Strasbourg Court on this
issue.[115]

4. The executive refuses without giving reasons

The same example from Poland about the 11 judges. The President
did not give reasons for his refusal. A TVN documentary showed
documents from the Presidents' Chancellery stating that revenge
on his adversaries was one of the motives for his refusal.[116]

5. The executive is refusing not just in quite exceptional
   circumstances[117]

The Luxembourg Court explicitly considered that
circumstances in which the Prime Minister of Malta refused
were 'quite exceptional'. An example of not so 'quite exceptional'
circumstances is the 11 judges in Poland: given that so many
judges, 11 of them, were refused more or less at the same
time, it does not seem to me to be an example of exceptional
circumstances.

6. The executive is refusing without the possibility of judicial
   review[118]

Earlier, I mentioned the systemic practice in Hungary of
annulling selection processes for Court Presidents where
the result was not to the liking of the executive. On 2 June
2021, the Hungarian Supreme Court ruled that there was no
judicial remedy against annulling a call for applications for the
presidency of courts.[119]

7. The executive is appointing while judicial review is still pending before a domestic court

The politically dominated selection body in Poland recommended seven candidates for the Civil Chamber of the Supreme Court. A number of non-recommended candidates appealed to the Supreme Administrative Court, contesting the legality of its recommendation. The Supreme Administrative Court issued an interim order staying the implementation of the recommendation pending examination of the appeals. The President of the Republic appointed despite the interim order. The Strasbourg Court ruled that the actions of the President were "in blatant defiance of the rule of law in order to render meaningless the judicial review" of the recommendation.[120]

In conclusion, the Hungarian and Polish cases seem rather obvious examples of undue influence by the executive over the selection process for judges. Systemically, probably, more interesting is the Iceland judgment. In that case, the Strasbourg Court imposed a Convention duty of very high-level reasoning on the executive in the case of a refusal to appoint a recommended judge, because the reasoning is not allowed to endanger the objectivity of the selection process. Judge Pinto de Albuquerque argues in his – on this point – dissenting opinion that the Court should have laid down the principle that the manipulation of the appointment of a judge to a court in violation of the relevant eligibility criteria is an absolute procedural error that cannot be remedied.[121] My question is, did the Court not, by introducing the duty – effectively – rule that the executive is only allowed to refuse a recommendation by a selection body on the basis of compelling reasons regarding the objective criteria (domestic law) of the selection process? I would argue that it did, but I agree with the judge that the Court could have been clearer on the matter.

4. CONCLUSION

Academic lawyers have an important duty to analyse, explain and criticize judgments of courts. This is, however, not the only duty of academic lawyers. They also have to identify problems in society and work on solutions for those problems. In the field of judicial independence this implies identifying – in an open dialogue with the European Courts and others - what next steps are necessary for the protection of independent justice in the European context of attacks by other state powers.

The work of the European Courts in this respect is quite impressive, but I am sorry to say not quite enough yet to safeguard the independence of the judiciary. In my opinion, the key to a long-term political control over the judiciary lies in political dominance over the selection and appointment processes of judges and Court Presidents. And this political control has to be stopped by all means. That is why I identified five next steps to achieve this. I will briefly sum them up:

1. Start filling the systemic enforcement gap
For a decade now, for political reasons, the Commission has failed strongly to enforce standards of judicial independence, contrary to its duty. This causes a systemic enforcement gap on a subject fundamental to the identity and functioning of the Union. The rule of law, furthermore, requires that judgments of courts are enforced by the executive. Therefore, on systemic grounds and in accordance with the purpose of the Union Treaties, the Luxembourg Court should contribute to filling the gap by imposing on Union Institutions a strict duty to enforce in

full, without delay and by all available instruments the judgments of the Luxembourg and Strasbourg Courts on the subject of judicial independence in the Union, especially, but not solely, on the subject of selection and promotion of judges, because this subject is most important for the executive to establish a long-term political control over the judiciary.

2. Enforce the enforcement duty effectively
In order to enforce effectively the duty mentioned under number 1, interested parties such as European organisations of judges should be allowed standing and legal interest by the Luxembourg Court for this purpose.

3. Give more effect to the standard of 'a majority of judges, elected by their peers'
A European common constitutional tradition is rapidly emerging as to the standard that the selection bodies for judges and Court Presidents should have a majority of judges, elected by their peers. The moment this tradition has been established, the European Courts must give effect to it. This effect should – at least – be that a selection body that is not composed in accordance with this standard is presumed to be under political control, unless proven otherwise.

4. Selection bodies must reason decisions
In order to be able properly to assess whether a selection process for judges and Presidents is in accordance with European law, the European Courts must demand from countries that selection decisions be reasoned, even if this is against the constitutional tradition of some countries.

5. Executive power to refuse recommended candidates solely on noncompliance with objective selection criteria

On the basis of the purpose of European law, the European Courts should make absolutely clear that the discretionary power of the executive to refuse recommendations of selections bodies for judges and Court Presidents is limited to noncompliance of these bodies with objective selection criteria. The refusal should give compelling reasons to this effect.

Mr Pro-Rector, ladies and gentlemen,

In conclusion, I would like to express my gratitude to the Board of Governors of Maastricht University for creating a chair for the Administration of European Justice in these difficult times for European judiciaries, and – even more so – entrusting me with it.

A special thanks goes to all my fellow judges and friends from all parts of Europe with whom I worked so closely for the last eight years to understand what it entails being a European judge and to learn, especially from Polish colleagues, what true courage and perseverance is made of in the fight for independent justice. Thank you for your trust, comradeship, wisdom and fighting spirit. I am looking forward to further cooperation. I am sure it will have more ups than downs in future.

I would like to mention four colleagues form the Dutch judiciary for their support and friendship when personal times were less happy. In alphabetical order: Marc Loth, Herma Rappa, Huib de Ruijter and my supervisor Jaap Spier.

In six of the last eight years I was able to be involved in European justice because my colleagues in the Netherlands' Council for the Judiciary graciously allowed me to do so. A special thanks to them. For the last two years, I mention the leadership, management and colleagues of the proud court of Zeeland-West-Brabant for their favourable support in facilitating my European work. Thank you very much.

Last, but certainly not least, a special thanks to my wife Liesbeth and children Lieke and Janne for their love and support.

Mr Pro-Rector, ladies and gentlemen,

I would like to end my inaugural speech with a *cri de coeur* on the basis of a quote of one of my favourite Hungarian novelists, Sandor Marai. It is about the betrayal and loss of friendship, but it might well refer to the loss of the independence of the judiciary. It goes like this:

It is not true that fate slips silently into our lives, it steps in through the door that we have opened, and we invite it to enter.

Ladies and gentlemen, I would like to make a strong appeal to you all to go the extra mile to close that door, in defence of independent justice.

I have spoken.

NOTES

1 The subject of this speech is researched until 1 January 2023.

2 First one I saw was in October 2022 in the Dutch newspaper *de Volks-krant*.

3 Art. 5 para 3 of the Protocol werving en selectie van raadsheren in de Hoge Raad der Nederlanden. (Protocol on the recruitment and selection of judges in the Supreme Court of the Netherlands), www.hogeraad.nl.

4 EC RoL Report 2022, The Netherlands, p. 3.

5 Just to mention some examples: Hungary and Poland to the detriment of judicial independence. *See* EC RoL Reports 2021, Hungary and 2020, Poland. Luxembourg and Czechia to strengthen judicial independence. *See* EC RoL Report 2022, Luxembourg and 2020, Czechia.

6 Polish and Romanian judges were not involved in the 2022 ENCJ survey. Polish judges, because the survey is done through the national councils for the judiciary, and the Polish Council for the Judiciary was suspended from the ENCJ as from 17 September 2018, and expelled on 28 October 2021, because it lacked the required independence from the executive. Romania did not participate. *See* ENCJ Survey on Independence of Judges (2022), p. 5, www.encj.eu.

7 Ibid., figure 31 on p. 35.

8 Ibid., figure 33 on p. 36.

9 Ibid., figure 32 on p. 35.

10 *See* David Kosar, Politics of Judicial Independence and Judicial Accountability in Czechia: Bargaining in the Shadow of the Law between Court Presidents and the Ministry of Justice, European Constitutional Law Review 13: 96-123 (2017) p. 122.

11 I define European law as the rights and duties based on the treaties mentioned.

12 ECtHR, *Grzeda v. Poland (Grzeda)*, 15 March 2022, 43572/18, para 324 and ECtHR *Juszcszyszyn v. Poland*, 6 October 2022, 35599/20, para 333: "The Convention system cannot function properly without independent judges."

13 *See* for instance the trial against Hitler in Patrick Dassen, De Weimar Republiek 1918-1933, Van Oorschot Amsterdam, pp. 386-390.

14 Art. 52, para 3, Charter of Fundamental Rights of the European Union (Charter).

15 Robert Spano, The Rule of Law as the Lodestar of the European Convention on Human Rights: The Strasbourg Court and the Independence of the Judiciary, European Law Journal, Volume 27, pp. 211-227 (2021), para 4.4 and Koen Lenaerts, The Two Dimensions of Judicial Independence in the EU Legal Order, Liber Amicorum L.-A. Sicilianos, Anthemis 2020, pp. 333-348, p. 348.

16 On 16 September 2022, Russia ceased to be a party to the Convention. The Russian invasion in Ukraine triggered this. *See* Media release Council of Europe Ref.DC 053(2022).

17 CT Poland 7 October 2021, K 3/21 (Art. 19 (1) TEU is incompatible with the Polish Constitution) and CT Poland 10 March 2022, K 7/21 (Art. 6 ECHR is incompatible with the Polish Constitution). *See* Adam Ploszka, It Never Rains but It Pours. The Polish Constitutional Tribunal Declares the European Convention on Human Rights Unconstitutional, Hague Journal on the Rule of Law (2022), doi. org/10.1007/s40803-022-00174-w.

18 *See* for instance the suspension on 25 February 2022 of Judge Anna Glowacka of the Krakow Regional Court, but there are many more examples mentioned on the website of the Polish judges association Themis under materials in English. https://themis-sedziowie.eu under the heading 'Materials in English'.

19 *See* the case law mentioned in para 3.2.3.

20 A bill to reform the law relating to human rights. Bill 1172022-23.

21 Lord Dyson, Human Rights Reform: A Dangerous or Welcome Change? The Justice Lecture Delivered by Lord Dyson at the University of Leeds on 16 November 2022, p. 15. *See also* Lord Manse, The Protection of Rights – This Way, That Way, Forwards, Backwards …, The Thomas More Lecture 2022, para 44.

22 I will not touch upon the subject of enforcement in the Council of Europe system, just mentioning problems in this field. *See*, for instance, Implementations of ECHR judgments: Annual Report 2021, Council of Europe, and Committee of Ministers, Supervision of the execution of judgments of the ECHR, Cases examined at 1451st meeting, 6-8 December 2022.

23 Art. 258 TFEU.

24 Art. 260 para 3 TFEU.

25 Regulation 2020/2092 of the European Parliament and of the Council of 16 December 2020 on a general regime of conditionality for the protection of the Union budget, LI 433/1, pp. 1-10.

26 Dawson and Muir characterized the 2012 infringement against the Hungarian 'judicial reforms' as technical and narrow in approach. Mark Dawson and Elise Muir, Hungary and the Indirect Protection of EU Fundamental Rights and the Rule of Law, German Law Journal 14 (10): 1959 (2013).

27 Matteo Bonelli, Infringement Actions 2.0: How to Protect EU Values Before the Court of Justice, European Constitutional Law Review 18 (1): 30-58 (March 2022), last sentence under heading 'The first attempts'.

28 Ibid., under the heading 'Infringements actions'.

29 And 23 other conditions regarding corruption. *See* written procedure completed on 15 December 2022 of the European Council, CM 5860/22.

30 Roger Keleman, Appeasement, ad infinitum, Maastricht Journal of European and Comparative Law 29 (2): (2022).

31 John Morijn, The Law and Politics of Protecting Liberal Democracy, Inaugural Lecture 2022, University of Groningen Press, p. 26.

32 Roger Keleman and Tomasso Pavone, Where Have the Guardians Gone? Law Enforcement and the Politics of Supranational Forbearance in the European Union, 2021, https://ssrn.com/abstract=399418. Forthcoming, World Politics 74 (4) (Fall 2023).

33 Grainne De Burca, Poland and Hungary's EU Membership: On Not Confronting Authoritarian Governments, International Journal of Constitutional Law 20 (1): 13-34 (January 2022).

34 *See* para 3.2.3.

35 Petra Bard and Dimitry Kochenov, War as a Pretext to Wave the Rule of Law Goodbye? The Case for an EU Constitutional Awakening, European Law Journal;27: 39-49 (2021). Wojciech Sadurski, The European Commission Cedes Its Crucial Leverage vis-à-vis the Rule of Law in Poland, Verfassungsblog (6 June 2022).

36 On 23 June 2022, the European Council granted Ukraine and Moldova the status of candidate to the European Union and set conditions for candidate status to be granted to Georgia; on 15 December 2022, it granted candidate status to Bosnia and Herzegovina, on the understanding that a number of steps are taken. *See* European Council meeting 15 December 2022 – Conclusion 30.

37 *See* for an example for Hungary para 3.2.2; for an example for Poland, *see* later in this paragraph.

38 And other rule of law aspects.

39 Regulation 2020/2092 of the European Parliament and of the Council of 16 December 2020 on a general regime of conditionality for the protection of the Union budget, LI 433/1, pp. 1-10.

40 Council of the European Union Implementing Decision on the Approval of the Assessment of the Recovery and Resilience Plan for Poland, reference number ST 9728 2022, 17 June 2022, p. 37 and Annex to the Decision, Section 1, Component F1, milestones F1G,

F2G and F3G. *See* for a summary Press release European Council, 17 June 2022, https://consilium.europa.eu.

41 Art. 52, para 3, Charter.

42 CJEU (Grand Chamber), *Commission v. Poland (Disciplinary Regime for Judges)*, 15 July 2021, C-791/19, paras 157 and 176.

43 For instance, using compliance with the duty as a precondition for payment of money from the Union Budget or Funds.

44 *See*, for instance, at the time when the Charter was not yet binding: The European Commission 1986-2000: History and Memories of an Institution, chapter 19, p. 483: "For the Commission … at least the proposals and decisions taken at EU level had to comply with it."

45 Art. 266 TFEU.

46 ECtHR, *Eminagaoglu v. Turkey*, 9 March 2021, 76521/12, para 134.

47 I disclose that I am involved in that law suit.

48 Consultative Council of European Judges, Report on Judicial Independence and Impartiality in the Council of Europe Member States 2017, para 16.

49 CJEU (Grand Chamber), *Repubblika v. Il-Prim Ministru (Repubblika)*, 20 April 2021, C-896/19, para 72.

50 At the time the Council for the Judiciary (KRS) with a majority of judges, elected by their peers.

51 *See* Case 35942/22, Borkowski, pending before the Strasbourg Court. *See also* Dariusz Mazur and Waldemar Zurek, So-called 'Good Change' in the Polish System of the Administration of Justice, 6 October 2016, p. 29.

52 *See* para 3.2.7.

53 Especially, the Presidents appointed by the Minister of Justice under his temporary special powers. *See* para 3.2.4.

54 CCJE Opinion No. 24 (2021), part I B paras a and c; Compilation of Venice Commission Opinions and Reports Concerning Courts and Judges, 5 March 2015, p 75; ENCJ Report on Councils for the Judiciary 2010-2011; OSCE-ODIHR Kyiv Recommendations on

Judicial Independence in Eastern Europe, South Caucasus and
Central Asia (2010), p. 3, Composition of Judicial Councils.

55 *See* OSCE, Towards a Culture of Accountability of Councils for the
Judiciary, 8 February 2021, para 3.4 (Georgia).

56 Ibid., para 4.2.

57 William Twining, Law in Context: Enlarging a Discipline, OUP 1997.

58 ECtHR (Grand Chamber), *Gudmundur Andri Astradsson v. Iceland
(Astradsson)*, 1 December 2020, 267374/18, paras 243-252.

59 Ibid., para 245.

60 Ibid.

61 ECtHR, Astradsson, para 243.

62 Lenaerts, 2020, p. 347.

63 Laurent Pech, The Rule of Law as a Well-Established and Well-
Defined Principles of EU Law, Hague Journal of the Rule of Law 14:
107-138 (2022).

64 For new members to the Union a transition period for limited time
might be considered.

65 BVerfG, judgment of the Second Senate of 5 May 2020, 2BvR 859/15,
paras 1-237.

66 ECtHR, Astradsson, paras 289 and 290.

67 Ibid., para 222.

68 Ibid., para 220.

69 ECtHR, Grzeda, para 262. Judges have a duty of loyalty to the rule of
law. I translate this duty into the requirement of courage.

70 ECtHR, *Besnik v. Albania*, 4 October 2022, 37474/20, para 103.

71 John Bell, Judiciaries within Europe, a Comparative Review, CUP
2006, p. 17.

72 Diversity here is defined as meaning that the composition of the
UK judiciary should reflect the society it serves as to gender, race,
sexuality and social background.

73 The Dutch Council for the Judiciary states that diversity furthers
the quality of the judiciary. Site of the Council under the heading:

'Maatschappelijk'. Internet site JAC: "We believe the judiciary should reflect the society it serves and we aim to attract diverse applicants form a wide field." Germany as well. *See* EC RoL Report 2022, Germany, p. 4.

74 House of Commons, Justice Committee, Oral Evidence of 29 June 2021, Judicial diversity Q6, 40 and 41: as to women 18% (2016) to 32% (2020); to minority communities 3.8% (2016) to 8% (2020).

75 Graham Gee and Erika Rackley, Debating Judicial Appointments in an Age of Diversity, Routledge 2018, p. 17.

76 *See*, for instance, Constitutional Reform Act 2005, Section 71 (panel for the selection of Chief Justice), Section 80 (panel for the selection of Justices of Appeal).

77 ECtHR, *Zakharkin v. Russia*, 10 June 2010, 1555/04, para 147.

78 ECtHR, Astradsson, para 245.

79 CJEU, Repubblika, para 57.

80 EC RoL Report 2021, Hungary, p. 5.

81 EC RoL Report 2021, Germany, pp. 3-4.

82 CCJE Opinion No. 24 (2021), part I B paras a and c; Compilation of Venice Commission Opinions and Reports Concerning Courts and Judges, 5 March 2015, p. 75; Recommendation adopted by the Committee of Ministers on 17 November 2010 (CM/Rec(2010)12, para 46; Parliamentary Assembly of the Council of Europe, Resolution 2316 (2020), para 7; The European Parliament, Resolution of 17 September 2020 (217/0360R(NLE)), para 24; ENCJ Report on Councils for the Judiciary 2010-2011; OSCE-ODIHR Kyiv Recommendations on Judicial Independence in Eastern Europe, South Caucasus and Central Asia (2010), p. 3, Composition of Judicial Councils.

83 ECtHR, *Reczkowicz v. Poland (Reczkowicz)*, 22 July 2021, 43447/19, para 265; ECtHR, *Dolinska-Ficek and Ozimek v. Poland (Dolinska-Firek)*, 8 November 2021, 57511/19 and 48868/19, para 283; ECtHR,

Advance Pharma v. Poland (Advance Pharma), 3 February 2022, 1469/20, para 321.

84 ECtHR, Reczkowicz, para 276.

85 Ibid., para 269.

86 Ibid.

87 EC RoL Report 2022, Luxembourg, p. 1.

88 EC RoI Report 2022, Czechia, p. 4.

89 EC RoL Report 2022, Spain, pp. 3-4.

90 The criterium is from CJEU (Grand Chamber), AFJR, 18 May 2021, C-83/19, paras 199-200. It is about management position on bodies competent to conduct investigations and bring disciplinary proceeding but is in my view equally applicable to Court Presidents.

91 Dariusz Mazur, Internal Affairs Department of the State Prosecution Service as a politicized tool of oppression of Polish judges and prosecutors, 6 September 2021, https://themis-sedziowie.eu under the heading 'Materials in English'.

92 *See* later in this paragraph.

93 ECtHR, Astradsson, para 245.

94 Mazur and Zurek, updated for 6 October 2017, p. 35.

95 2,000 days of lawlessness, Report Free Courts, 23 June 2021, p. 12.

96 In this case, the President of the National Office for the Judiciary, appointed by the Hungarian Parliament.

97 EC RoL Report 2020, Hungary, p. 3.

98 EC RoL Report 2022, Hungary, p. 5.

99 EC RoL Report 2022, Austria, p. 4.

100 ECtHR, Astradsson, para 230 'including by the executive'.

101 EC RoL Report 2020, Italy, p. 3. The case was about the selection of chief prosecutors, but the same selection body deals with the selection of judges and presidents of courts

102 In Italian: 'correnti'.

103 L. 17 giugno 2022, n. 71 (1).

104 Constitutional Court of Georgia, *Public Defender of Georgia v. Parliament*, 30 July 2020, N3/1/1459, 1491 paras 38-56.

105 Kyiv Recommendations on judicial independence in Eastern Europe, South Caucasus and Central Asia (2010).

106 OSCE, Towards a Culture of Accountability for Councils of the Judiciary, 8 February 2021, para 4.3.2.

107 CJEU (Grand Chamber), *A.K. and others*, 19 November 2019, C5895/18, para 123; CJEU, Repubblika, para 57.

EC RoL Report 2021, Hungary, p. 5.

EC RoL Report 2021, Germany, pp. 3-4.

CCJE Opinion No. 24 (2021), part I B paras a and c; Compilation of Venice Commission Opinions and Reports Concerning Courts and Judges, 5 March 2015, p. 75; Recommendation adopted by the Committee of Ministers on 17 November 2010 (CM/Rec(2010)12, para 46; Parliamentary Assembly of the Council of Europe, Resolution 2316 (2020), para 7; The European Parliament, Resolution of 17 September 2020 (217/0360R(NLE)), para 24; ENCJ Report on Councils for the Judiciary 2010-2011; OSCE-ODIHR Kyiv Recommendations on Judicial Independence in Eastern Europe, South Caucasus and Central Asia (2010), p. 3, Composition of Judicial Councils.

ECtHR, Reczkowicz, para 265; ECtHR; ECtHR Dolinska-Ficek, para 283; ECtHR, Advance Pharma, para 321.

ECtHR, Reczkowicz, para 276. Ibid., para 72.

108 For instance, the NVVR, the Dutch Association for the Judiciary.

109 ECtHR, Astradsson, para 263.

110 ECtHR, *Xero Flor v. Poland*, 7 May 2021, 4907/18, paras 277-278.

111 CJEU, Repubblika, para 70.

112 ECtHR, Astradsson, para 264.

113 CJEU, Repubblika, para 73.

114 2,000 Days of lawlessness, Free Courts Report, p. 5, mentions ten judges, but the court case eleven. Since 2018, the judges in the

selection body are elected by the Polish Parliament. *See* earlier in my speech.

115 *Case of Borkowski v. Poland*, 35942/22.

116 Mazur and Zurek, updated for 6 October 2017, pp. 29-30.

117 CJEU, Repubblika, para 72.

118 CJEU, A.K. and others, para 145.

119 EC Rule of Law Report 2022, Hungary, pp. 4-5.

120 ECtHR, Advance Pharma, paras 323 and 345.

121 ECtHR, Astradsson, para 11 of the separate opinion of Judge Pinto.

www.ingramcontent.com/pod-product-compliance
Lightning Source LLC
Chambersburg PA
CBHW061127210326
41518CB00034B/2552